Let's Eat Lunch

Lisa James
Photography by Siân Bradfield

Contents

Lunch

Let's eat lunch!
What do you have for lunch today?

pasta
sushi
noodles

Sandwich

I have a sandwich for lunch.
My sandwich has salad and cheese in it.
I made it myself.

bread
butter

Salad

I have a Greek salad for lunch.
The cheese in my salad is called fetta.

My salad is made with lettuce, tomato, cucumber, onion and olives.

Sushi

I have sushi for lunch.
My sushi is made with rice,
cucumber and seaweed.
It's easy to make and
it tastes good.

cooked sushi rice

cucumber

seaweed

1. Put the rice and cucumber on the seaweed.

2. Roll it up.

Pasta

I have pasta for lunch.
My pasta has tomato
and onion.
I eat my pasta slowly
because it is hot.

1. Cook some chopped onion in oil.

2. Carefully add tinned tomatoes.

3. Stir in cooked pasta. Now your pasta is ready to eat.

Noodles

I have noodles for lunch.
I eat my noodles with chopsticks.
Noodles are fun to eat.

My noodles are mixed with chicken and vegetables.

Fruit

We have fruit for lunch, too.
Fruit is healthy and it tastes good!

oranges
grapes
watermelon
banana
apple
Did You Know?
We should all eat two servings of fruit every day.

Picture Index